# Social Media Encourager

Also By
Mary Alayne B. Long

A Mother's Prayers For Her High School Son

# Social Media Encourager

A collection of
Humorous, Helpful & Heartfelt
social media posts

Written and Curated by
Mary Alayne B. Long

An imprint of Everything Southern Press

Social Media Encourager:
A Collection of Humorous, Helpful and Heartfelt Social Media Posts

Written and Curated By: Mary Alayne B. Long

First Edition 2023

Library of Congress Control Number 2023905325

Paperback ISBN: 9798385652747
Hardcover ISBN: 9798386696009

Printed in the United States of America

Social Media Encourager

www.thealabamahousewife.com

# Introduction

Social Media. It's an interesting term. And if we look to Webster's Dictionary we will find the following:

Social: adjective; Relating to society or its organization.

Media: noun; The main means of mass communication regarded collectively.

Relatively simple definitions, right? Yet when you put those two words together it can sometimes feel like we need a new Schoolhouse Rock to teach us all what in the world is going on. I honestly think that if the little man driving the conjunction junction train could see how some of us behave when draped in the anonymity of the online cloak he would go on ahead and plow that cute little train straight off the rails.

I often wonder if people know that the things they write and post and share can actually be seen by others. It can be rough out there y'all. Pretty darn rough. I prefer to ride the cute little steam engine that tours about through the real life, joy-filled communities that are (thankfully) getting more attention on social media these days. They're out there, I promise. Sometimes you have to be on the lookout because "happy" doesn't always get to drive the algorithm train. In reality though, there's a whole lot more good than bad to be found.

Back in 2020 when the wildfires were ravaging the Australian landscape, a comedienne named Celeste Barber set a goal to raise $30,000.00 to help with the recovery efforts. Before you could say koala, she raised over $51,000,000.00. That's fifty one M-M-MILLION. Out in Utah there is a family who rallied the whole world to fast and pray for their daughter who was recovering from Leukemia and for days on end over 150,000 people all over the globe had sweet Indy Llew at the top of their prayer lists. All because of the power of social media.

I do my best to restrict my own social media sharing to those humorous, heartfelt and helpful stories I believe can give someone a smile. And I also set aside time each month to cull the accounts I interact with; making sure I steer clear of those who are overly curated, posed, styled, and anyone who's sharing hurtful or harmful rhetoric. I especially can't stand to see accounts that clearly paid for followers. It's sort of like going to a dinner party and being seated at a table filled with mannequins. What's the point? I want to see the good, the bad, and the ugly that goes along with really real life. It is the things we have in common that bind us together. Not the things we pretend to be or to have.

I know there are tons of great guys who beautify social media in many different ways and I love that. So much. However, I think the women of our world have a special responsibility to use our own social media presence to share the stories that truly need to be shared. The ones that are the reverse of clickbait. The stories people wouldn't be drawn to but still can't turn away from. We have to share them because we are the listeners. We are the secret keepers. We are the watchers. The ones with eyes on all the balls being played in games that don't always draw a crowd. We have to open the eyes and ears of those who need to see and hear what is good.

We must bring people together to make the world a better place for all of God's children. And all we need is love—and maybe a phone. And a voice that speaks the truth.

On the following pages you'll find a collection of my old posts that I've pulled together just for you. They are not in chronological order—or any sort or order for that matter—but I have grouped them in into four categories: Observations, Sentimental Journeys, That Photography Class I Took and Personal Perspectives. Lordamercy that sounds like a list of odd Jeopardy categories.  Anyway…. I hope they will encourage you to smile. I hope they will encourage you to learn. I hope they will encourage you to be a thoughtful person. And above all else; I hope they will show you the good side of social media and in turn encourage you to be a bright spot in someone else's day.

All the best to all of you,

Mary Alayne

Social Media Encourager

www.thealabamahousewife.com

# Let's Get Started

# Include Everyone Period

If this is your first introduction to me; I thought it would
be helpful to share a few things you need to know. If
you're old hat, you can flip on through to the next page
as you clearly already know what kind of crazy you
signed up for. For starters I want you to know that I
chose the shirt for this picture because in my social
media space I do all I can to include everyone. Period.
Unless you are an awful person who is mean for no
good reason and then I will ask you to politely excuse
yourself find and find a better use of your time. If you
do land in the "new reader" category here's what you
need to know: First of all, I believe in God, The Father
Almighty, maker of Heaven and Earth.

I love Him with all my heart and do all I can to put Him first in everything I do. I also love you even if that's not the path you find yourself on. I love America, so much, but how you treat children, old people and dogs matters to me far more than your politics.

I have little to no patience with rude behavior and parents who don't discipline their children make me insane.

I was born and raised in Alabama and when my children flew the coop my husband and I moved to Florida—which we absolutely love. However, you should have no doubt, I will always be FROM Alabama. Roll Tide!

I am also a Southern humorist, a storyteller, a home training expert, a wannabe philanthropist, an interior design enthusiast and I absolutely adore British period drama.

As a storyteller, social media is only one of the ways I share my work. My life is a big part of that work so you will see and hear a lot about my family there.

On the other hand, my work is not my life—so there's far more I keep private. My husband and I also make a lot of crazy videos. Sometime's they are about cooking. Sometimes they are about etiquette. Sometimes they are simply clips of me sitting in my car ranting about how people don't return their grocery buggy to the store or why they can't properly maneuver a four way stop or why tourists walk down the street in swimsuits without a coverup. (I will NEVER understand that one.)

And all of that to say…..

I am all over the place— in a focused yet scattered sort of way. And I'm a lot—in a polite yet loud and excited sort of way. So if you're looking for a planned out, filtered, staged life—I may not be your cup of tea. And that's okay. Maybe you'll stick around to give me a chance and maybe you'll bring along a few friends. For those of you who've been with me a while and to all of you who are new, I am very glad you're here. All of you. And I am just tickled to have you along for the ride.

# Observations

Social Media Encourager

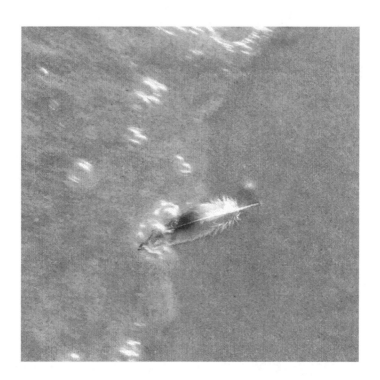

www.thealabamahousewife.com

# The Feather

I stood and watched as the water crept closer and closer, hoping to get this shot. Then the wave washed over the feather and swallowed it up out of sight. Only for a second. Then I saw it again and picked it up expecting it to be wilted from the water and covered in sandy grit. Instead, it was like a fresh, clean feather that had just fallen from the sky. All the dirt and grime were gone. So weird. It made me think of how we can be at our worst and then end up better than we ever imagined when we let God lead the way.

The feather reminded me that He doesn't lead us into deep waters to drown us but to cleanse us. Don't be afraid of what He has in store for you. Jump in. Into the deep end. Swim out past the rope. Dive down and touch the bottom. You'll come out fresh and clean on the other side. I guarantee it.

www.thealabamahousewife.com

## Sideways

Pocket call. Accidental photo. Sorry, that text wasn't for you. How often do we make careless mistakes when we are in a hurry? Or not paying attention? Or doing seventeen things at once? Or all of the above? Pandemonium and murder (hornets and sadly, actual murder) and riots and you name it have consumed our lives. Not unlike this picture (accidentally taken by Daddy) the early days of 2020 seemed rather sideways. And all of them beckoned us to slow down and take stock of the world we've all allowed to sprout up around us. We have failed to properly tend this glorious garden that we have been granted from God almighty and I'm sad to say it's horribly overgrown. It's time to pull out our boots and garden gloves and start pulling up some weeds. Because if we don't get at these problems by the root they'll only multiply and resurface. So let's all be more intentional with our thoughts and our words and our actions and our time. There's a beautiful picture in the making and I can't wait to see the finished product.

www.thealabamahousewife.com

# Be So Good

Not long ago I spent the day in Franklin, Tennessee
and as I walked up and down Main Street bobbing in
and out of quaint little shops I found a sign that read
"BE SO GOOD they can't ignore you." I couldn't help
but think it was a reflection of the entire town as
everyone everyone I encountered greeted me with a
friendly smile. They all seemed like "good people."
Every last one of them. Now, had I sat down with a
group of them for any length of time I have no doubt
we would have found things we didn't agree on, and
that's fine. Sometimes as we scurry through life and
mindlessly scroll through our various social media feeds
we forget that we really are surrounded by nice people
most of the time. We miss it because we have an eye
out for discord. We look for folks who aren't like us so
we can tell them how wrong they are and make them
feel bad all while claiming to show them the way. Our
way, that is.

The truth of the matter is "our way" doesn't matter one hill of beans. We are all supposed to have different opinions and differing views but what we are NOT supposed to do is get mired down in our differences and personal views so deeply that it takes our eyes off of the real work we are supposed to be doing—God's work. Of course, I don't believe we should sit idly by as we watch people mistreat others or break the law. But if we can learn to disagree without being disagreeable then perhaps we might even draft a few new folks to the team. We can't simply know Jesus ourselves and stop there. He didn't say….Follow Me and don't tell anyone else where we're going. He said….Follow me and blow a trumpet and twirl a baton and shine a spotlight so nobody can miss this parade! He wants us ALL marching together. Matthew 5:16 tells us "In the same way, let your light shine before others, that they may see your good deeds and glorify your Father in heaven." Not glorify other people. Not glorify yourself. Glorify God. So let's all find a way to walk together. We don't have to hold hands, but if we will all simply BE GOOD; it won't be something that can be ignored.

And PS—I'm wearing majorette boots and I totally get to twirl the baton.

Social Media Encourager

# Cows

On my regular drive from Alabama to the Florida I go down lots of back country roads. I always say I'm going to stop and take pictures of the cotton fields or the old barns or the cows but I never do. I'm always in a hurry and tell myself "next time" but—that time never seems to come. Last week, I drove right on past those pretty little cows yet again but this time I turned around and went back. I pulled off the side of the road, grabbed my camera (which I always take because I always plan to stop) and I climbed up a briar covered hill in the rain—while wearing flip flops. I scared them away at first but coaxed them back over (small town Alabama girl knows how to call up some cows) for a quick photo session and then I was on my way.

I'm not into resolutions but this year I have resolved to live. That's it. Just live. Live where I am. Live in the now. In the actual moment. Live the best way I can for the time that I'm in. To show up and be where ever I am. Really be there. Because being present matters.

And because my friend Brian Erickson told me that attendance doesn't necessarily equal presence. Today at church we talked about how The Wise Men came to see Jesus when nobody else did. They didn't even belong there. They were different. They were astrologers. Just some groovy guys who saw a cool new star and decided to follow it.

They chose to be present in order to worship the new born King. They showed up. Today I was reminded that we've become people who choose albums over concerts, ESPN over the actual game and screens over people and this year, I pray that we will take a deep breath in, put the phones down, and make time to show up. Let's stop to smell the roses, listen to the music or even to pull off the side of the road and call the cows. Let's BE where ever we are. And let's give all our thanks to God along the way. He's the One who ALWAYS shows up.

And before you start, don't @ me about the cows. I love them. I wanted to pet them. And I'm well aware I could never be a farmer. Let it go.

Social Media Encourager

# My Messy Closet

Yesterday I posted a picture of our kitchen sink covered
in coffee grounds and other "mess" that should have
found its way to the trash can. My husband didn't care
for it and couldn't believe I shared it. I explained that I
thought it was funny and I wasn't trying to social media
shame anyone. I also explained that sometimes folks
like to see the mess behind the curtain. The really-real,
non-staged, less-than-magazine worthy photos of life that
make us feel a little less less-than. But that's another
story for another day. I deleted it because it bothered
him and I have a strict "Humorous, Helpful or Heartfelt
only" rule I try to stick to for Instagram. He then
threatened to take a picture of my messy closet and post
it, all in good fun of course. And all of that started me
thinking about how often we all misinterpret intent
because we don't TALK to each other. Written words
(especially short, snappy texts) don't always convey the
author's accompanying emotions properly.

We owe it to ourselves and those we surround ourselves with to talk more. We aren't helping anyone by jumping to conclusions and flying off the handle about things we don't completely understand. Especially when we don't have all the facts. So everybody take a breath and have a chat. Talk about how your day was. Talk about how you feel. Talk about how I posted a picture of my horrible closet because that's just how really real it is around here right now and say how awful I am for letting it get so messy. Whatever floats your boat. But just TALK. And learn to LISTEN. No keyboards or judgement allowed.

Social Media Encourager

# Black Eyed Susans

I drive by this roadside patch of black eyed susans every day and yesterday I told Sadie Sue that I keep meaning to pull over and take pictures of them. She looked right at me and said "What's stopping you?" Dad gum those smart sassy children we raise to be just like us......

What would we do without those wonderful mirrors in front of our faces reminding us daily who we are supposed to be? So let me remind you to stop. Take the picture. Smell the flowers. Be yourself.

# Vision

Do you see a flower or a weed? How we see things depends on what we look for. Are you looking for happiness, or discord. Do you respect other people's views or are you looking for an argument? Can you appreciate things you don't understand or do you think everybody who isn't exactly like you is crazy?

The world will present you with many choices—but YOU are the one who has to choose. Choose joy. Choose understanding. Choose patience. Choose to see the flowers.

# Choices

In life, we don't always get to choose our circumstances.
Sometimes we get to take the ride.
Sometimes we get to tow the boat.
Where ever we sit, what ever our view; we should
remember that a kind, helpful, glad and joyful heart is
always an option.

We may not get to pick what's put in front of us, but we
can sure as heck decide how we will view it.

Choose wisely my friends.

This is not my photo. I'm not sure where I found it but
I would imagine it originated with The Birmingham News. I can't swear to it though.

# Four Little Girls

Today in church, we were reminded of the day The
Sixteenth Street Baptist Church in Birmingham,
Alabama was bombed. On that morning, Addie Mae,
Denise, Carol and Cynthia were on their way into the
sanctuary to hear the children's sermon about the Love
that forgives when they were struck down by a bomb
that took out every piece of stained glass except for one
—the picture of Jesus The Good Shepherd.

This morning, our pastor pondered how many of the
Christians living in Birmingham at that time pretended
that racism was not their sin, that racism was not their
problem. And I can't help but wonder how many of us
are still pretending today.

I was not alive in 1963 but when I look back at the
photos and read the stories of the days surrounding The
Civil Rights Movement, I'm sorry to sound crass but—it
literally makes me want to vomit.

It is hard for me to comprehend that the place I called home for over a quarter of a century was once filled with such hate and overwhelming ignorance. Those people were so dad gum blind. My gosh—how on earth could they have been so lost?

It is up to ALL of us to squash hate when we see it. And we must follow Dr. King's suggestion to meet the forces of hate with Love. It's not always an easy path to walk but when we look to God to show us the way, His Amazing Grace will allow us to see all things clearly.

God Bless those precious girls. May their memory always bind us in love.

Social Media Encourager

www.thealabamahousewife.com

# Jesus

I parked on a city street the other day—something I've
done a million times before. Never thinking twice about
it and certainly never paying one bit of attention to the
ground in front of me. This time, when I walked back
to my car, I noticed the lines on the pavement formed a
cross. It was clear as day right there in front of me. A
perfect white cross. It literally stopped me in my tracks
and made me start to think about how many times
Jesus sits and waits for us to notice Him. In today's
world where people fight over things that really don't
matter, where children go missing, where life (to some)
has lost its value, where love is often stored up in jars
rather than shared with those around us and where
people are entitled and greedy and rude.....I wondered
how often to we fail to see Jesus when He is right there
in front of us, just waiting for us to take a single step. A
step toward Him. A step toward kindness. A step toward
love. A step toward a life like no other.

So during this joyous, holy season let's keep our eyes focused on The Cross and let's look for Jesus in unexpected places. He's there, waiting for us to take that step.

Social Media Encourager

www.thealabamahousewife.com

# In Or Out

Are you staying inside; over on the shady side of the
street? Or are you out and about; living your best life in
the sunshine? This image struck me as I walked
through the empty pathways of Seaside yesterday and
made me think of how we've become a bit divided
lately. After all the time of togetherness during our
respective quarantines, when we insisted we would all do
better and be better and live better lives—now we are
back at it. Nipping at each other about masks and
gloves and when to get a haircut and who to believe.
The media is not helping. They love to stir the pot and
now they've made such a huge mess on the stove it's
going to take a while to clean it up. So I say to you—as
I usually do—Read. Research. Learn. Adjust. On your
own. Do what's right for you and your family. Check on
the people who can't go outside. Share what you can
with someone in need. Learn to disagree without being
disagreeable. Go out to eat or stay in and cook. Your
choice.

It's okay if you're scared. It's okay if you're not. You are free to stay in the shade or stand in the sun. Use your common sense. And for the love—be nice to each other. Karma will come to visit sooner or later and only you decide if she comes bearing cruelty or kindness.

Your choice.

Social Media Encourager

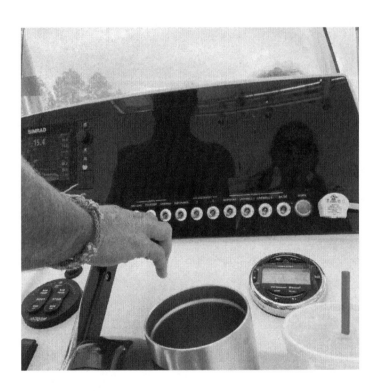

# Reflection

So many crazy things seem to be swirling around us right now. It can feel overwhelming and troubling and tempers flare. Mine included. And I think it would be a really great time for all of us to reflect on our own lives and to stop finding fault with everyone else's. When is the last time you volunteered at a homeless daycare center? When is the last time you shopped for groceries on behalf of a needy family? When is the last time you offered to cut the grass for an elderly neighbor? When is the last time you dropped off supplies at a women's refuge? When is the last time you took food to the animal shelter? When is the last time you donated to charity? Or sent in your tithe to church? How are you using your life to make the world a better place for someone else?

Before we get caught up in pointing out what everybody else is doing wrong, let's make sure we have done all the good we can for all the people we can as often as we can.

Words on a screen, no matter how sincere or well intentioned, aren't doing any good if we don't back them up with action. Turn off the news. Put on a smile. Be a helper.

Social Media Encourager

www.thealabamahousewife.com

# Blending In

This pretty little moth has been hanging out on our
front porch for a couple of days now. No doubt hiding
out from the seemingly crazy world we are all making
our way through these days. A world we are all to blame
for, by the way. We've been sitting by and taking the
easy road for far too long. Letting sports and leisure
activities replace our religion. Letting our desire to be
liked and loved replace our ability to make smart
decisions. Letting our fear of dealing with inconvenient
situations replace our commitment to discipline our
children. And letting ourselves believe that we alone are
enough. We aren't. And we've all been fooling
ourselves. We can't hide out any longer. We've got to
take the reins and get the mule plowing straight again.
(Country girl reference. Y'all know what I mean.) We've
got to make hard choices. And difficult decisions. And
we've got some pruning to do in this fallen garden we
all live in. If God gets his hands on the hedge clippers
before we do it's not going to be pretty.

And I'll tell you right now—no matter how hard we try there's no hiding from Him.

Social Media Encourager

www.thealabamahousewife.com

# Toxic Masculinity

If you are overly troubled by toxic masculinity;
you're hanging around with all the wrong men.

# Forgotten

I came across these shoes on my morning beach walk.
No doubt left behind and forgotten by someone who
I'm sure loved them and wore them well. Perhaps
someone running to escape the storms blown in by the
hurricane as it quickly changed paths and headed our
way. I can see it in my mind....a family gathering up
their children, folding up chairs and umbrellas, bagging
up beach toys and starting on that hike back to the
house. Moving so fast they even forgot their shoes.

I think sometimes we can start to feel a little bit like
these much loved shoes—forgotten. It's a feeling
everyone struggles with from time to time, no doubt.
And while the people walking on this earth may not
always leave us feeling loved, The One who made this
earth won't ever leave us at all. And He will always love
us. He may not always love the things we say or how we
act. No doubt. Yet He will always point us back to Him
when we wander off the path and forget to put Him
first.

We would to do well to remember that when we find ourselves mired down and covered up in worry or fear or loneliness or regret or sin or whatever—that's on us. We are the architects of our own misery. And it's our job to dig out of the pit, shake off the sand and move our walking feet back in the right direction. So if you're feeling alone and forgotten today, know that I'm thinking of you, and praying for you. And know that even when the storms of life come your way; The One True God is always by your side.

# Fishing

Daddy left out early this morning and fished until well after lunch. One catch and release after the next until he landed that pretty little redfish on the right. He called in a happy mood to say he was headed home with supper and I was so glad he'd enjoyed the day. When he was pulling the boat back in he called me out to bring him a knife and decided he'd drop a line in off the wharf while he waited. Before I even made it out, that big redfish on the left took the bait. I got there just in time to snap this picture and it really made me stop and think. So often we sail around in circles thinking we might be missing out on something when in reality, the best things in life are often right at home. So think long and hard before you decide where to cast your line. You might miss out on some really big fish right in your own back yard.

www.thealabamahousewife.com

# Loaded Down

I followed Daddy home from the beach the other day
and when we stopped at a red light I got tickled at all
his manly stuff in the back of the truck surrounding a
very girly pink and green Lilly cooler so I thought it
would be funny to snap a pic. But then when I started
looking at the picture it made me think about all the
mental and emotional stuff we haul around with us in
our lives. The thoughts of folks who lied or cheated or
did us wrong—or God forbid did something to
someone we love—can take up a lot of space. And the
hours we spend thinking of ways to get them back do
too. Whooooo Lawd I love to plot revenge......

But we alone decide what to keep in the car trunks of
our hearts and the truck beds of our minds. And some
people are driving around in U-Hauls—especially after
a year like 2020. So take some time today to clear out
the trash. Hose things down. Pull out the vacuum. Have
a good clean out and scrub everything down.

Let go of all the mental and emotional junk that holds you down—and be merciless.

Pretend to light it all on fire if it makes you feel better. Taking responsibility for cleaning up your own mess can be tough work but gosh almighty you'll feel better when you're done. And once you get things straight—stop letting the folks who screw things up for you go for ride-alongs in your life. Take charge of YOU.

Then you can put on your coolest pair of sunglasses and cruise through life with a much lighter load.

Social Media Encourager

www.thealabamahousewife.com

# Fill Her Up

The sweet little man who keeps Baby Blue running like she should tells me I only need to burn a particular brand of premium gas in her. Nothing else. He says she won't run right if I don't. So I drive miles out of my way to get to the right gas station and so far she hasn't let me down. Last time I drove over I started thinking about what we use to fill ourselves up—mentally and physically. I mean, if I can go out of my way for a forty something year old car why wouldn't I do the same for my fifty something year old self? So I'm trying harder to spend more time with God—-THE MAIN SOURCE of all good and great things. I'm trying to make better choices about what I put in my body & what I put on my skin & what I put in front of my face. I'm spending more time outside.....in bare feet whenever possible and doing all I can to fill myself up with good food, good friends and good times. I'm working harder to grow my writing career and finding new ways to increase my audience and to keep y'all coming back for more.

I'm letting go of the bad "fuel" that creeps in from time to time. Sometimes that looks like turning off the news. Sometimes it looks like saying "no" and sometimes it looks a little like selfishness to others. I can't do anything about that. People will see what they want to.

All I know is I'm grateful for this life I've been given and with every day that passes; I'm closer to the end than the beginning. So I'm letting the top down and I'm cruising toward the sunset with the knowledge that I'm not going to waste a single minute on anything or anyone toxic. And you shouldn't either.

Social Media Encourager

# Rewind

I wrote this back in 2017-right after the fiasco in
Charlottesville, Virginia—and today, it felt right to share
it again. So here goes....

I simply can't sit quietly by for another single minute.
I am appalled at what I have seen on television today
and you should be too. Shame, shame, shame on every
single being (I stop short of using "human being" as I'm
not sure they qualify.) who participated in the fear
fueled, hate mongering display of complete and total
ignorance that took place in Virginia today. While I
support freedom of speech and assembly and
understand it is a two way street; this situation simply
boggles my mind. As a life long Southerner let me
assure anyone who is confused—these people do not
represent me, my region or anyone I have ever met in
my entire life.

To be clear, in The South:

We love Jesus and we still love YOU even if you don't.

We have pride but we aren't boastful.

We drive trucks and we drive Mercedes.

We are fiercely loyal, especially to our family, friends and neighbors; and we will always lend a helping hand to ANYONE in real need.

We are educated on farming and Shakespeare. We aren't all racist or homophobic. We understand the real meaning of charity. We don't all live in trailer parks and we don't judge those who do.

We will be in church tomorrow morning praying for God Almighty to lead our country and our citizens to a peaceful end to the hatred that has taken a strangle hold on our society.

And to be very, very clear—We do not support, condone or abide by any sort of terrorism— foreign or domestic— and we will NOT stand idly by while evil, corrupt groups of villainous fools attempt to use our towns as bully pulpits to spew hate. This is not who we are and this is NOT my South.

I can't even imagine what The Reverend Doctor Martin Luther King, Junior would say about the world today. I'm not sure I want to know. But I'll tell you what I DO know—I know I believe in a better South. I believe in a better America. And I believe in a better world. For everybody. I only pray we will all learn to follow Dr. King's example of Love.

And I hope it's not too late.

# Sentimental Journeys

Social Media Encourager

# My Favorite Actress

This may be my all time favorite picture of Sadie Sue. Ever. She was eight years old and we were at The Waldorf in New York City for her birthday. A friend called and asked me to meet "a guy" in the lobby to look at some knock off bags for her and when he showed up he had a huge black trash bag of purses. Not the least bit suspicious at all. While I was on the phone with her trying to relay the situation, Sadie Sue was convinced we would be carted off to jail at any moment. So-- she put on the leather jacket we purchased that day, grabbed my glasses off my head and a candy cigarette from the Dylan's Candybar bag and hid behind a plant. Some folks may be surprised she's pursuing a fine arts degree in theatre--but not me.

I saw this coming from a 100 miles away.

# Otis

On Sadie Sue's third birthday, we got Otis. I took her to
pick out her favorite little poodle at a cute little old
lady's house and when we got there, all the puppies
were running around playing except for one. He was
laid back in the shade underneath a chair so she
crawled right under there with him and they were joined
at the hip from day one. Last week I knew his time was
getting close. On Friday, I knew he was ready. So I held
him while we danced under the full moon and a million
stars, Daddy and I drank a toast to him, then I put him
on my chest for the night. I didn't sleep. At 1:45 I lit a
candle and laid a small, special wooden cross next to it.
I prayed for God to take him straight to Papoo when he
got to Heaven and I sat there until the sun started
coming up. Then I walked outside and whispered the
words of "Surely The Presence" in his ear and a few
minutes later, still in my arms, he took his leave. I
bathed his face and wrapped him in his favorite blanket.
Daddy dug a perfect grave down by the water while I
watched out the window.

I printed out pictures of him with Sadie Sue and with all of us and put them in the little box with him—and we buried him together. We used a cross that Jake made for me years ago and I gathered azaleas and a palm branch from the yard while I was still in my nightgown. We were both crying like fools. And it was precious.

We still have three wonderful, beautiful, amazing dogs and we love them every bit as much as Otis. But Otis was the first. He ruled the roost. He was the King. Daddy and I have surprised ourselves by the way we have mourned this dog so deeply. You'd think we didn't have actual children. Or that we'd never stood over the grave of a dearest loved one. It's been so strange. I've cried more in the last three days than I have in the last twenty years. And if you know me—you know the only emotions I allow in my life are joy and anger. And oh my gosh I loathe crying. So much. But he is worth every single tear and I'll miss him more than I can possibly say.

Social Media Encourager

www.thealabamahousewife.com

# Love

I could wax poetic about Paul and his lovely letter to the
Corinthians though I think we've all heard those
promises before. We know all about love being patient
and kind and how it doesn't boast or turn green with
envy, etc. etc. And while I'd never presume to contradict
him I will say I think there's a few other things to
consider. Sometimes love is loud and sometimes it's
quiet. Sometimes love is fun filled and sometimes it's
lonely. Sometimes it comes easy and sometimes it's hard
work. It can mean taking care of someone and it can
mean leaving someone to care for themselves. It can
mean helping someone move to a new house and it can
mean letting them live their own life. It can mean
asking about someone's day and it can mean not
mentioning a word about it. On occasion, it can mean
people thinking you're crazy when they find you
drinking pink champagne on the porch in your
housecoat with a big 'ol redneck and it can also mean
watching that same redneck digging a grave for you dog,
in the rain, at six o'clock in the morning and standing

by you in reverence and sorrow as if you were burying the Queen of England. (Nope—still not over it. Soon though, I think.)

Love is so many different things for so many different people. The one thing I know that's always true is this; love—real love—is a choice. And it all comes from The Lord. That means it will never lead us to hate or harm another one of His children. Not ever.

So as you eat your chocolate candy and sip your own champagne be grateful for the people in your life who show you their love in all its many colors. The ones who love you, and the ones you get to love back.

Social Media Encourager

# The Light Switch

This switch-plate cover was in my nursery when I was a baby and stayed in my room for years. And years. When Sadie Sue was a baby it made the move to her bedroom but recently I swiped it back. It's now proudly mounted in my new closet and every time I flip the switch it makes me happy. *Sentimental Hoarders* unite and shine the light on the small things that make you happy!

Be smart, keep things neat and don't be irrational about it. (Side Note—If you need a storage unit for your memories you may want to get some perspective—and some professional help.) But don't let anybody else be in charge of telling you what you get to keep and what you have to throw away. YOU decide what makes you smile.

www.thealabamahousewife.com

# Fancy

I loathe made up, commercialized Hallmark
Holidays....and Mother's Day is near the top of the list.
I do love my mother though—-quite a lot—and I think
she may actually own stock in Hallmark. She's all in for
anything and everything sentimental, loves to go places
and do things and see people and gather up family
members in large groups and is likely the nicest person
you'll ever meet. She also spends a good deal of her
time trying to figure out where I came from and why I
could not possibly be more different from her. I'm not
sure we will ever figure that one out but this photo is
evidence that she is at least partially responsible for my
high level of sass.

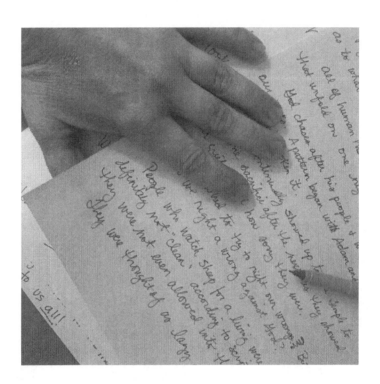

# Church

Sometimes, you stop packing and cleaning and making beds to turn on the radio and listen to your pastor talk about Jesus. You sit in your Christmas pajamas with paint covered hands and use a cardboard box top for a lap-desk to take sermon notes. And you get reminded about how unworthy you are and how that doesn't matter to God because He sent Jesus anyway. You learn about how unworthy the shepherds were. And you learn to pay attention not only to the things angels say—but also WHO they say it to. How would that important message have trickled down if that angel had sought out the "right people" to tell first? The Good News is for EVERYONE. Divorced, Depressed, Disbelieving, Downtrodden? Doesn't matter.

The Manger is in front of us all. Come and see with your own eyes—then go and SHARE THE GOOD NEWS! For to you, and me and even the grinchy guy down the street—A Savior Is Born! Pass it on....

# Bloom

About 15 years ago, I noticed the neighborhood
landscapers pulling up all the buttercups after they had
bloomed. They were tossing them in the trash bin so I
stopped and asked if I could have a few. That afternoon,
they delivered a huge black trash bag of discarded
flowers, bulbs intact. We planted a row of them out
front and they've never failed to reappear each year
since. In Alabama the weather is crazy so you never
know when they'll show up. I thought I would miss
them this year since we sold the house but when I
pulled in the drive yesterday afternoon (I'm here for a
week to clean this place out for the darling new owners)
they were here to greet me. It's a reminder for me to
never cast aside anyone who may seem less than or all
used up. God's power to renew us is never ending. He is
always faithful and He put all of us  here to help tend
this garden of people we meet every day. So be on the
lookout for someone who might need your help to
bloom again. A good garden is full of all sorts of life.
And the possibilities are endless.

# The 105

Do y'all know what that means? I didn't until 2013
when Jake moved into Bryant Hall four days after high
school graduation. No senior trip. No fanfare. Just a
long, hard, hot summer as a Walk On at The University
of Alabama. That's when I learned that only 105 players
make "The 105." Those are the ones who spend two
grueling weeks at camp. Those are the ones who get to
dress out for games. Those are the ones who travel.
Those are the ones who get to be in the team picture.
So when he left for college and wrote "Make The 105"
on his bathroom mirror; I never could bring myself to
wash it off. And you know what? When he was a senior,
after three years as a scout team player who was full of
determination and grit; he made the cut. Not because
he was chasing a dream. Because he was working toward
a goal. And he's still working. And he still has his eyes
on the prize. And he will probably kill me for writing
this because he's humble and takes compliments worse
than I do.

But I'm chancing it anyway because I think it's a great example to anyone who knows what they want and is willing to go out and get it. Whatever you're working toward—keep grinding. Keep planning. Keep making yourself better. Keep on keeping on. It's worth it.

Aim Small. Miss Small.

(And PS—the new owners are going to have to clean this mirror. I can't do it.)

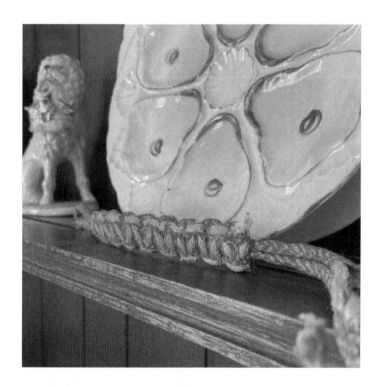

# The Bracelet

Rick Long has had this bracelet on his arm for nearly ten years. As you may have guessed—he is not a bracelet kind of guy so—there have been several occasions when he's been questioned and even made fun of for wearing it. Yet once he tells the story of how our son, when he was younger, made two bracelets for each of them to wear; people start to understand. When he follows that up by telling them how his father passed away quite unexpectedly a day or two after, and how Jake sent his own bracelet to the funeral home to go on Papoo's wrist instead of his own and how no matter what anyone has ever said he would never cut it off— they really get it. And most often they end up shedding a tear while joining him in a toast to Papoo.

Yesterday the hospital told him he would have to cut it off before his hip replacement surgery. He explained. They understood. But sterile operating rooms are non-negotiable.

So this morning, I very carefully and tediously (and miraculously) found a way to untie it. He was beyond relieved. And I've placed it on a little shelf where we have lots of pretty things to keep it safe. And while it may not be the loveliest of treasures to anyone else; it's one of the most precious things he owns. And the memories it provides are priceless.

Social Media Encourager

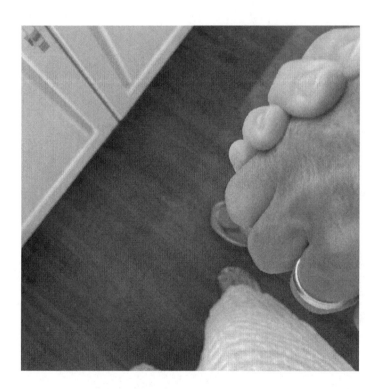

## Saying The Blessing

Every night before we eat supper —and before any meal we share—we hold hands and pray. At home. In a restaurant. On the beach. Where ever. (If we are at home we also close it with a little kiss.) If you've ever sat at a table with either one of us you know we're gonna' pray before we eat. The end. Tonight, when Daddy said the blessing, he covered all the standard bases, Jake, Sadie Sue, our parents, other family and friends and of course—our country. He asked God to guide our steps and our understanding of those we disagree with. And then, before he gave thanks for the food, he said "and God, please be with The Ginsburg Family" —and it caught me off guard. Because he's not really one to keep up with current events. And he doesn't have a ton of patience with things or people he doesn't understand or agree with. But right there in our kitchen, in front of me and God and the dogs, he set an example we can all follow.

You can disagree with someone and still respect their authenticity and dedication to their beliefs as well as the positive impact they make on the world. And you can honor their life. So if my big ol' redneck can be nice, you can too.

You know, every night after he prays, he always says "that was a good one, wasn't it Mama?" And tonight my verdict is a resounding yes.

Social Media Encourager

# The First Day of School

This was Sadie Sue's first day of kindergarten. Daddy
followed us to school that day snapping pictures the
entire way. (It was Jake's first day of sixth grade as well
but he was far too cool to hang with us on our walk.) It
was also a time in our lives when he was miserable at
work. They were changing things up. He was traveling
three and four days a week. He had less control over
how his customers were handled. And he hated
everything about the place he had loved for more than
twenty years. We talked about it a lot. We prayed about
it even more. Then one night he came home so
bedraggled and exhausted and I looked him straight in
the eye and said "I don't care if we have to sell our
house and you have to start cutting grass for a living.
You've got to quit." And I meant every word.

After we walked back home from dropping Sadie Sue
off that day he drove to work, went in, told his boss he
wasn't going to miss watching his children grow up,
cleaned out his office and never looked back.

No idea where or when the next paycheck would come. No idea what he'd do next. But strong faith in God and a clear idea of what kind of father and husband he was going to be.

Thankfully, God led him to a wonderful job where he stayed until he retired. He kept this picture on his desk until his last day and now it lives on his bedside table. A simple reminder that when you put God first and family second you'll always end up walking down the right path.

Social Media Encourager

www.thealabamahousewife.com

# Mr. Berryhill

I am going to announce something that will be pertinent only to people who have never met me: I am an only child. And while there were a few days back in the summer of 1978 when I wished for a brother or a sister; I have never really felt like I missed out on anything. I reveled in my only child-ness and enjoyed most every minute I spent growing up in small town Alabama with my wonderful parents. My mother was a banker and my daddy taught school so during the summer months I usually spent more time with him. He would let me drive down the dirt roads near my Aunt and Uncle's farm. He let me go barefooted and always said "yes" to the hot fudge cake for dessert, even at lunch. I was fortunate indeed that he didn't stop for a single minute to think that he couldn't teach me about woodworking or car repair or painting or plowing or anything I ever wanted to learn simply because I was a girl.

When I was little, and the snow came through in the winter, my daddy would cart my friends and me around to sled on all the great hills until we were too frozen to move. Then he would make us all hot chocolate, put our gloves and socks in the dryer, and take us back out again. On hot summer afternoons he would let us ride in the back of his truck to get snow cones at the Tasty Dip. He literally created the first ever "mash up" for the First United Methodist Church Candlelighter's Choir when he taught us to sing Oh How I love Jesus and Jesus Loves Me at the same time. We called it Orange Juice, which made absolutely no sense at all—but he let us. And we loved it.

He can play anything in the world on the piano—by ear — and was the lead singer in more than one very hip 1960's band. He sang at our wedding reception while my husband and I danced to Color My World and then proceeded to shut the place down with me as we did an entire father-daughter dance routine to Wooly Bully. Lordamercy knows if You Tube existed back then we would have gone viral. I look back on all those fun times and I am so thankful he taught me all the things he did. Even though I was a girl, it never occurred to him that he shouldn't.

Because of him I know to keep my eye on the ball when swinging a bat and my thumb on the outside of my fist when throwing a punch. I know to measure twice and cut once. I know to always treat a gun like it's loaded. I know how to negotiate when buying a new car. I understand how to take responsibility for my actions. I know if you act like you know what you're doing you can get away with just about anything. I fully grasp the importance of helping others any chance you get. And I know how to hold my own pretty much anywhere I go.

I have tried to pass along what I learned from my parents to my children— who could not be more different from each other. They seem to have listened and learned fairly well through the years and like most parents, when I see them use a skill I taught them it gives me a great sense of accomplishment. Especially if it's something my daddy taught me first.

So if you have children, remember that little folks are watching you. They want to learn what you have to teach, and you should let them. Boys can learn how to hunt and how to cook a great meal. Girls can twirl batons and hang sheetrock—even with a pink bow in their hair. Whatever you choose for your children, never forget that there's not much in this world that can equal the life lessons you learn from a parent who truly loves you.

www.thealabamahousewife.com

# Old Picture

I came across this picture today while I was doing a little cleaning and I can easily say it's one of my faves. We were just sitting there having a cocktail and talking about life and watching the sunset when a friend offered to snap this picture. There was no thought about posing or setting it up. We just looked over at her and she clicked. With an actual camera—not a phone. No "let me see" or "take it again, please" followed. Only a thank you for noticing us and making the offer to capture the moment.

It was eleven years and two jean sizes ago. And he still wears that shirt.

He's also still smitten—and so am I.

And I hope we're still living in the moment like we were then. I think we are. At least I hope so.

So here's to old pictures, stolen moments, sunsets, cocktails and of course, The Flora-Bama. Oh—and to real cameras. Can we please bring those back?

Social Media Encourager

# That Time I Took
# A Photography Class

Social Media Encourager

# The Candelabra

This week, our photography class' lesson was about illumination. We were given the task of "finding the good light" inside our homes. Our instructor told us to get rid of all artificial light and to remember that the closer we are to the source of illumination, the better the glow. I took this photo last night as it became dark outside. It is totally un-altered, there's no filter in use and I have to tell you, I took several shots because I couldn't believe how much light was coming off of the candles. (I'd also like to say I got all the way down on the floor to snap this and I'd like some applause. Not so much for getting down there but for getting back UP!) When I thought about Martin Luther King, Jr. Day tomorrow, it made me think about the light he used to illuminate the world and his famous words reminding us that darkness cannot drive out darkness—only LIGHT can do that.

I'm back in Birmingham now and as I sit here typing this, only miles from the very jail where Dr. King penned his famous letter and closer still to the Sixteenth Street Baptist Church, I am thankful to have lived my life close to people who cast a lovely glow on this world. I hope one day I can find a way to be the good light in the life of someone who needs it. I pray that God will allow me to rid myself of the artificial lights in my life and that He will keep me close to those who seek to serve Him by loving others. May He guide my way with His never ending source of perfect illumination.

www.thealabamahousewife.com

Social Media Encourager

# The Lay Flat

My photography class is supposed to be working on a
"lay flat" picture this weekend. We were instructed to
choose things that matter to us, lay them all out flat, and
then focus on color, lighting, editing and all that goes
along with creating a picture to represent your life and
who you are.

I chose— *My Bible, stuffed with bulletins that are
covered in sermon notes. *Books from both my
children, filled in with the sort of love and kindness that
makes you feel (even if only for a moment) that they
actually DO know what all you do for them. *A "Love
You More" freehand cross stitch piece from Sadie Sue.
*A tray I love and a rock Jake gave me when he was
three or four. *A good candle and some matches. *An
Alabama Football shaker that's traveled far and wide
with me for years. *And I framed it all around the
happy face Sadie Sue carved into the dining room table
when she was little.

When I worked on editing I got things looking pretty good—I think. And then I did a second version in gray tones as well. It reminded me that whether the world is coming at us in full living color or plain old drab black and white, if we will just be still, or "lay flat" with a focus on the things that matter, it's easy to remember that everything's gonna' be alright.

Social Media Encourager

# The Place Setting

I'm playing a bit of catch up with my photography class
assignments this week. Today, I'm "leaving something
out" of the picture—that's why it's off center. But I love
it still because I love pretty dishes and glasses from any
view and I really enjoy setting a lovely, lively table. It
makes me smile. I have more China patterns than the
law should allow but my favorite pieces on this table are
the hand-me-down dinner plates. They belonged to my
Maw-Maw and when she passed away a few years ago,
nobody wanted them. But I did. They aren't from
England or France and I doubt they'd fetch much at an
estate sale but they are worth their weight in gold to me.
Every morsel of food that's ever been served on them
was prepared by her hands and was filled with love.
(And bacon grease, I'm sure.) I remember them so well
from the special times we would sit at her dining room
table to celebrate with the ones we love and looking at
them now, mingled with my own wedding china, makes
me feel connected to her in a way I can't quite describe.

Thinking about my Maw Maw and the great meals she prepared conjures up memories of lunch on a stool at her kitchen counter along with a plate filled with turnip greens, corn bread, pinto beans and a window unit air conditioner keeping us cool while we watched The Price Is Right.

If you can relate to times like that you're my kind of people.

Either way, set aside some time to drag out your favorite dishes and cook a good meal for someone you love. Mix and mingle and spice things up. And if you can find a way to include someone who might feel a little bit left out of the picture, that's even better.

Social Media Encourager

# The Dice

Today the assignment for my photography class is about "depth of field" and I was instructed to find an interesting background and then photograph the subject of my choice, setting space between the two, to create a layered image. My background is a picture of Papoo. The subjects of my choice are his dice. The thoughts of a man who could hunt, fish, garden, play cards and shoot dice better than a professional gambler-- all while never failing to put God first and family second--have me cruising down memory lane with the top down and a Johnny Cash song on the radio.

He paid his way through The University of Alabama working nights and used his first paycheck to buy his mother a set of silver. Silver we still eat with every Thanksgiving and Christmas. He adored his dogs and his grand children.....not necessarily in that order.... and loved to have a good time better than anyone you've ever known. He was layered, to say the very least.

And even though I know he's likely sitting around right now watching Andy Griffith reruns with Andy Griffith--and Bear Bryant too—the selfish part of me is not always fond of the space between us and would love to have him back. Even if only long enough to snap a good picture.

Social Media Encourager

# The Wedding Flowers

Photography class is back in session and this assignment
finds me rifling through my "favorites" folder for
something in my past that gave me a new perspective.
And so I present to you............Laura's Flowers. Last fall
my sweet friend got married on a Tuesday afternoon in
a beautiful mansion in Tennessee when it was about 21
degrees outside. I am not a florist and I don't even play
one on TV but I did, nonetheless, put together her
wedding flowers and trucked them (duct taped into chic
fi a cups) all the way from Birmingham to Nashville.
When I unloaded them into The Bride's Room I sat
them all down in the first empty spot I could find. That
happened to be a windowsill and I stopped to take a
picture—not because I thought they were anything
special but because there was just something about the
light coming through the window on that cold, cold day
that made me feel warm inside.

Maybe it was the bridesmaids all scurrying around in the background. Maybe it was the overwhelming feeling of love that filled that entire afternoon. Or maybe I was just having a hot flash. Who knows.

What I do know for sure is that Laura has given me a new perspective on a lot of things—and flowers are only the tip of the iceberg.

Social Media Encourager

# The Silver

My current photography class duty is to share a picture
of a collection—gosh my teacher sure does make every
assignment such fun! Trouble is, I'm not a collector.
The closest I get is likely with china and sterling silver
but I really love silver. Really. The olive spears and ice
cream forks and baby spoons and jelly servers and salad
serving sets thrill me to no end. And I don't believe in
keeping things packed away for something special that
may or may not happen either. I even wrote a column
about silver a few years ago and I use mine everyday.

I hope you'll take this as a suggestion to make every day
special. Whether you use silver spoons or plastic forks
doesn't matter. It's the people you surround yourself
with that make all the difference and to be sure,
Professor Kelle Hampton is welcome at my table any
time.

# The Camera

I'm taking another semester of photography this fall and I'm focusing on re-learning how to use my actual camera rather than the camera on my phone. For far too long, the convenience of grabbing my phone for quick, easy pictures has kept me from something I love —my camera!

Today I am working on a project using natural, indoor light—focusing on side light and shooting from above. So,.....this is me, standing on my island in my nightgown, taking a picture of my beloved camera during an early morning reunion. I'm so ready to put this blasted phone down and reacquaint myself with her and learn new ways to slow down and capture the lovely moments of life that can be lost in the daily hustle and bustle.

For me, sometimes that means pictures of my children. Sometimes pictures of the dogs. Sometimes it's a sunrise or a flower or a flock of pelicans or a fish Daddy caught or even a stack of firewood. Whatever catches my eye and fills my heart with happiness and beauty.

So if there's something special (or someone, maybe) that used to make you giddy with excitement and you've let the crazy, fast paced, I-want-it-NOW world blur it in your mind; use today to pull it (or them) back into the spotlight. You will be so very glad you did. I promise.

Social Media Encourager

# The Dog Bowl

My current photography assignment finds me learning
to study natural light in my home. Leave it to me to
choose the dog food bowl as my subject. Another way to
confirm I'm weird, I know. Add it to the list. But as I
watch d the light change and thereby change my view as
it passed by Otis' leftovers during the course of the
morning; it really made me think about life.
(*See "weird" above.) Sometimes when we think we are
in a dark place all we need to do is shift perspective and
look for the light.

www.thealabamahousewife.com

# Personal Perspectives

# Chit Chat and Me

Matthew 18:2-3 says....... And Jesus called a little child unto him, and set him in the midst of them, and said, "Verily I say unto you, except ye be converted and become as little children, ye shall not enter into the kingdom of heaven." It is easy to read only those two verses and believe that Jesus wants us to be care free and spend our days playing around having fun like small children. But here--as is so often the case--context plays a huge role. As the disciples began to squabble about who would be second in command, Jesus wanted to teach them about dependance and humility. And he wanted them to stop fussing about things that didn't matter.

Small children do not have any achievements or accomplishments. They don't crave authority. They are easily teachable and willing to learn. They are trusting. They are humble and forgiving and they are completely dependent on their parents for care.
They are free from sin.

Jesus wanted His disciples to listen, learn, and to depend wholly on Him and He wants the same from us. He wants us all to know that the senseless squabbling we often engage in is only a deterrent that keeps us from seeking Him. As long as we keep Him in first place; second, third and all that follows won't really matter. It all falls into proper order.

On this lovely Sunday, I pray that we will all become simple, humble followers of Jesus and that we will see Him through the eyes of a child.

(PS-That's Chit Chat The Cat. He is the greatest cat that ever lived. Ever.)

Social Media Encourager

www.thealabamahousewife.com

# Big Mood

I've been in a glump all day and I'd really love to punch
somebody dead in the face right about now. Not Daddy
—he's been incredibly accommodating—I suspect
because he is a little bit scared. But I do have my eye on
a few people in Washington D. C. who I'd dearly love
to get after with a spanking spoon. I also have the
feeling I'm not alone in that. The overwhelming barrage
of (insert ugly cuss words here) that's hurled at us every
day is getting to be a bit much. I've also been working
really hard on my health the last few weeks and have
only lost two pounds so that's part of it. I won't lie. But
y'all know me. Y'all know I love Jesus and that my
Hope is built on nothing less. Still, that doesn't always
give me the ability to ignore the world as it seems to
explode all around me. Funny thing is, if I didn't have a
television or a phone I wouldn't have a clue what's been
going on these last few months. Where I live it's
business as usual. Smiling faces. Friendly chats.
Neighborly visits.

And I mean, I live at the beach for goodness sake. How can that put somebody in and ill mood?

I'm so much more grateful for that than you'll ever know, by the way. So I guess what I'm saying is....If you love Jesus and you live a great life and you have a million bajillion things to be thankful for—you still get to be in a mood once in a while. Don't let anybody tell you otherwise. You don't need to feel guilty about it either. You can be as mad as you like. Just don't let it change you.

Do something about it. Get you a baseball bat and go out to the junk yard to beat up old cars. Chop down a tree out in the back yard. Go underwater and scream. Put the top down and drive fast and blast The Violent Femmes. Whatever it takes to shake it off and keep it from settling in. But give yourself a moment. Or an afternoon. Try not to burn anything down if you can help it and find a positive way to use your energy as quickly as possible.

But don't you dare think you're all alone with your mad. I assure you my friends, you most certainly are not. In the end, when all else fails, look to Mr. Rogers. He knows what to do with the mad that you feel. Because let's face it; Mr. Rogers always knows what's best.

Social Media Encourager

www.thealabamahousewife.com

# Proud

Surely it will not surprise you to learn that I have
many dear friends who are a part of the gay community.
If it does surprise you, or if you have a problem with
that, you are perfectly welcome to excuse yourself
without comment and catch up with me later. Or not.
Your choice. And I will remind you that in my personal
social media space, I curate it as I alone see fit.
It is not the place you get to say mean things
or be rude....especially to people you've never met.
So there. Now that we are all clear on all of that, let's
continue....

I'll start by telling you that of my friends who happen to
be gay, some have always known they are gay. Some
struggled really hard with the realization and suffered in
ways that make me sad even now. Their origin stories
aside, I would have missed out on so much without
them in my life.

I never would have had the most amazing wedding pianist. I would have missed so many fantastic beach days and road trips and late night monorail rides at Disney World and fabric buying excursions and cocktail parties and concerts. Even a bar fight. So... pretty much life in general. Most of them are loved as they ought to be by their family and friends. Yet even today, in 2021, I'm sad to report I also have friends who've been shunned and cast away by the very people who are supposed to love them the most.

It saddens me to think that there are people who claim this sort of hatred and betrayal all in the name of Jesus. I don't know where they grew up in church but I grew up learning and believing that Jesus is LOVE. Not hate. The things we've done in His name to drive our friends in the gay community away from church make me want to spit up. Even if you believe that being gay is a sin (And to be clear—I do not.) how on earth can you think it's worse that any of your own? I love Jesus with all my heart and Lord knows I sin every day before my feet even hit the ground. I sure am glad nobody decided to tell ME I'm not welcome at church. Y'all know I'd go anyway because I don't let other people interrupt my personal relationship with God. You shouldn't either.

And you sure as shit don't have any business telling ANYONE that God doesn't love them. He does. He loves us all. And He wants us to love each other. He wants us to build lives and families and communities that serve Him. We can't do that if we are casting aspersions about each other and being hateful.

So let me just close by telling you that I'm proud to have friends in the gay community. I love them and God does too. Plus, they make my life so much more colorful!

# Firestorm

I've started a few in my time and that's not likely to change any time soon. However, in recent weeks I seem to have kept that fire pit extra hot and I've had folks blow on out of here in droves—after announcing their departure of course. Of course.

Anyway—people got really mad at me on two occasions: Once when I wrote about how much I love my friends in the gay community (and how much God loves them too) then once again when I shared a photo of sweet, precious Sophia Sanchez wearing the same shirt I have on in this picture. Lordamercy that one set off a pretty big spark. When I talked about this shirt and the reason behind it's creation I got mean messages about how I shouldn't be "political" and how I was horrible for this reason or that. It was my first hate mail so it surprised me a bit but didn't discourage me at all. I promise I can out mean anyone else and I guarantee you don't want to test me.

I was simply interested to learn that 1. There are people who think using the "R" word to describe our friends in the special needs community is political and 2. Other people think they can be the boss of me. Both are laughable at best and both are quite wrong. Bear in mind I am not one of those "words are violence" people. They're not. They're words. That's it. Still, they can wound even those with the toughest skin.

I will forevermore defend the rights of free speech AND I want us all to remember we are responsible for every single word that comes out of our mouths. Lord knows I've said plenty I shouldn't have. No doubt. With age I've tried to learn how to think long and hard about the things I say. And the things I write. Some days are easier than others....... However, I'm doing better and I hope you'll make the same effort. At the very least, I think we can all agree that the "R" word has long since passed the age of retirement and it's high time to let it sail on off into the sunset. Moving forward, let's all remember how impactful words can be, especially here on social media. Use that power for good. Use words that include and uplift and show love. It's easy if you try. And please don't give me a reason to be mean to you. You will not like it. I promise.

Social Media Encourager

# Wes Anderson

The times the three of us get together these days are few and far between and the things we all have in common are fewer still. But give us a Wes Anderson movie any day of the week and we're sold. So when we sat down to take this picture (at my insistence because it will likely be Christmas before we're all together again) and Jake said "We're The Extraordinary *Charcuterie* Of Individuals Alike" I fell out laughing and our quick simple photo op turned into an impromptu Wes Anderson movie poster photo shoot. Not everybody would get that. But we do. (And to be clear, he said "charcuterie" rather than "coterie" because he knew it would crack me up.) When we got up to keep walking through Ruskin Place, I pinned it all in my mind as a memory that would be on the top of my list for years and years to come. It's the weird things that connect us. It's our shared sense of humor. It's the unplanned, out of the blue moments that drop into my lap when it's just the three of us. And I love that more than you'll ever know.

# Brunch

As so many of you have very generously donated to the
Ruby's Rainbow 321 pledge this month, I've had lots of
questions about why I'm so involved. I'm not completely
sure I know exactly why. I guess it's like most other
things—because they let me. What I am completely
sure about is this: Last month, we hosted a brunch for
several mothers of children in that community and as a
part of the morning they all took 30 minutes to sit alone
and write letters to their child (or children) born with
Down syndrome. It made me more grateful than I can
say to be able to offer a place of quiet solitude for them
to gather their thoughts. Afterward, as they came
together to share what they had written, Daddy and I
tried to be quiet as we straightened up the kitchen but
couldn't help hearing them read their letters aloud. The
hopes, dreams and fears they expressed sounded a lot
like many of my own. We are all most certainly more
alike than different. It was both heart wrenching and
heart warming to be listening in and we all had tears
streaming down our faces. Yes, even Daddy.

I feel very led to be a voice on the other side of the special needs community. Well, not on the other side but on the edge of their circle I guess. One who says "Yes—I see your child. Yes—I love your child. Yes— your child is invited." All the "yes" things that mothers need to hear. That's what I'm here for. I will not be a voice of "no" in this community and I won't sit idly by as other un-educated souls continue to misunderstand Down syndrome.

Just last week, some guy at a park hustled his daughter away from my friend's little boy and wouldn't let her play with him.......and we are all grateful to Jesus I was not there or I might be typing this from the jail house.

The truth is, all mothers have fears and while I know there are certain things that go along with raising a special needs child that I've never had to worry about, the truth is those of us who haven't been blessed in this way need to do a better job of letting these mothers know we are on their team. We need to bring them into OUR circles and love on them just a little bit more.

Let's take away some of those fears and tears by cultivating a better world where we ALL know that Down syndrome is nothing to be down about!

Social Media Encourager

# Nashville

Not too long ago I took an impromptu day trip to
Nashville. I flew in and out and got busted at security
for having water in my purse. I still think the glasses are
what got me pulled aside but once you commit, you
commit. All I know is—it was one of the wildest,
craziest, most fast paced days I've had in quite a while.
And it was absolutely wonderful. I would do it all again
just to spend time with some of my most favorite people
in the world.

All of them have two things in common-
1. They are all crazy enough to be friends with me.
2. They all have at least one child with Down syndrome.

If you've been here for more than two seconds, you
know I have a special love in my heart for the Ds
community. The amount of pure joy they bring into this
world is clearly a God given gift they each carry within
them.

If you already know about Ruby's Rainbow and Jack's Basket and Brett's Barn and Sandal Gap Studio and The Rise School and Clemson Life and all of the wonderful places that are making a HUGE impact for them I'm glad. If not, do me a favor and check them out. You'll be thrilled. You'll be amazed. And you'll be filled with Joy. I have no doubt.

And I'll tell you right now—
there's nothing down about it.

Social Media Encourager

# A Barefoot Easter

Easter Sunday found me barefoot and in slacks.
Something that definitely would not have happened
under normal circumstances. I guess you could say it
was a "modified version" of Easter. And while the four
of us hovered around my laptop in the den to watch
church, I couldn't completely let go of the formality that
normally accompanies the day. I wanted us in our
Sunday best. I wanted us all on the same pew. And I
wanted us all sitting together for a meal. All things that
couldn't take place this year given the circumstances.

I decided to make the best of it and pulled out a mix of
old family china and crystal to remind us of the ones we
didn't get to see and I cooked way too much food and
we sat and ate and talked and laughed and set off the
fire alarm (Daddy never thinks to turn on the fan when
he tries to fry things.) and we all had the best time.

Then everyone napped and watched TV and played
with the dogs and then we did it all again for supper.

Except we ordered take out and used paper plates for supper. And the unusual, quarantine Easter quickly became my favorite. Even cleaning up the kitchen seemed fun. Because this is my wheelhouse. This is my happy. As much as I love and adore writing and storytelling, being a mother will always be my first choice when it comes to an occupation. Housewife is an easy second. Nothing brings me joy like taking care of my family. I hope and pray when all this is over, and we whiz back into our Zoom free lives, the world won't loose sight of what truly brings us happiness and joy.

SPOILER ALERT—it doesn't come from Amazon. Or Target. Or TJ Maxx.

And I trust that we all take this as a lesson from God to train our sights on Him. He is always there waiting for us. To pay attention. To be grateful. To celebrate the promise of Easter. And to love each other. He never gives up on us and He has all the faith that we will learn to sit together nicely without fighting—and learn to clean up our messes.

And I'll tell you something else—He doesn't do modified. He doesn't change. He doesn't leave. He sits and waits in love for all of us to come home.

Social Media Encourager

# Blurry

If I'm honest, I have to tell you that I set up my phone
to snap this picture this morning so I could see just
exactly how fat I am. True story. But when I looked at
the picture and saw it was blurry I was glad. Nobody
wants to see me in a swimsuit. Truly.

Then I started thinking about another kind of blurred
vision. You know, the kind we get when we let our
minds be clouded with one sided information. Like how
we so often see what we want to see instead of what's
really there. It's the view we get when we believe
everything we hear as long as it suits our own purpose.
It's how life looks when we don't do the work and the
research to find the truth that so many would dearly
love to keep hidden. When we wrap ourselves in
blankets of left and right and politics and rhetoric and
hate and violence when the only thing that will really
keep us safe and warm at night is God.

So try to find your focus. And make sure you start by looking at Him. If you seek to serve His agenda (which by the way is nowhere near hidden) first before all else I promise you'll have a whole new view of our world. You'll start to see things clearly. And that's a beautiful sight.

Social Media Encourager

www.thealabamahousewife.com

# My Clogs

I've had these clogs since college. And they've literally
walked more miles with me than I can count. We've
been through two pregnancies (when nothing else felt
right on my feet) and multiple Disney World trips and
countless football games and walks through Central
Park and the streets of San Francisco—you name it.
So while the world keeps spinning I keep clogging
along. Thankful for the simple things, like an old pair
of shoes that make me feel like me.

And I don't know what does that for you—maybe it's a
hat or a pocket knife or your grandmother's brooch or a
pair of shoes your Daddy drove you to Poppagallo to
buy when you were still a teenager. But I hope you have
it. I hope you're grateful to God for the memories it
brings. And I hope it makes you smile.

# Recluse

These days I rarely wear shoes. A house dress or—as
the days get warmer—a swimsuit and a cover up are my
favorite costumes of the day. And it's not uncommon for
a week to pass by without me ever finding myself
behind the wheel of a car. Home is my happy place and
it's filled with slow motion mornings and laid back
afternoons. There's not a whole heck of a lot that I need
or want to do that I can't take care of right here. I've
pretty much always worked (as a mother and as a writer)
from home and I'm very happy to continue.

I am trying to branch out just a bit and I've got lots of
great things and some really exciting trips coming up in
the next few weeks. But I wanted to let you know that if
you like staying home best, there's nothing wrong with
that. Nothing at all.

And go ahead and know that an empty nest can be
amaze-za-za-zing. It's certainly not anything to dread, I
can assure you.

So if you find yourself in my....well, I can't say "shoes" because I'm not wearing any....so I'll just say "place." If you find yourself in my place, let yourself enjoy it without any guilt. Life's too short for uncomfortable clothes AND uncomfortable situations.

HOME is where the fun is.

Social Media Encourager

www.thealabamahousewife.com

And now I'll close it out
with the post that started it all.......

www.thealabamahousewife.com

# Social Media Encourager

I loathe the term "influencer." It sounds like another name for a drug pusher to me. And really, isn't that what those people do? They drug you into believing you need what they have, get you hooked on ridiculousness and leave you begging for more.

I have long said I am not trying to influence anyone to do anything except to use nice manners, to be kind and to have a good time. So in this space, I ENCOURAGE people—to laugh out loud, to be happy, to be healthy, to be generous and thoughtful, to cook good food, to live well and to enjoy life.

I use my voice to share humorous, helpful and heartfelt stories that you (hopefully) will want to share with your friends.

I tell funny stories and talk about pretty things and making a home and raising children and what real life really looks like.

I do my best to use the gifts God gave me to entertain and uplift everyone who's nice enough to give me a few minutes of their day.

And I want to be sure you know—I am so glad you are here! I want to encourage YOU to look for the good and the happy. There's so much of it out there—even on social media.

I promise.

Social Media Encourager

# Author's Note

If you're still here after all of that I clearly owe you a
thank you. Otherwise I'm not sure I have much else to
share right now and I surely don't want to run y'all off
by over staying my welcome. I do think it's worth
mentioning for the new readers here (because I started
to wonder if you may be confused) why I mention
"Daddy" so often. I call my husband Daddy. He calls me
Mama. We've always done it. It's Southern—just go
with it. And I want to be sure you know—although I'm
certain there is little to no doubt—all of the photos
(except for one) are mine, they were all taken by me or
someone I love and appear here in their original form.

Except— they're all black and white here, as color
printing is rather expensive and I didn't imagine anyone
would want to fork over fifty dollars for this book.

Social Media Encourager

However, if you find you simply can not go on without the color versions of said photographs and if you also find you have money to burn; there's a hardcover edition available that will provide you with each and every photo (except for a couple that were black and white to begin with) printed in glorious full color form and you are most welcome to purchase one if you so choose.

I also want you to know that in reading back over these old posts as I edited this collection I was surprised at the number of times my words speak to my faith. I am not a Christian humorist, storyteller or writer but I am a humorist, storyteller and writer who's a Christian. I guess that bleeds into my work more than I realized and I am not the least bit sad about it. If you follow me on social media you know that for several years I have started each day by publicly sharing a Bible verse. In private, I start each day with prayer and a devotional. Sometimes I even look up old sermons on YouTube and watch one while I lie in bed. Suffice to say, my faith is my foundation. Even when it may seem to be in the background it is the beginning of everything I do. And while I fail miserably in many ways to live the life that God wants for me—I am trying.

I would sincerely love the words you have read here to encourage you to take stock of those you engage with on social media and perhaps even lead you to abandon accounts that thrive on divisiveness. Hate comes in many forms and when you allow it in your daily life it starts to blend in. And that's not good.

Finally, I hope this collection reminds you that the words we choose each day are just one big construction site. They can build up or tear down. Our conversations matter and they reflect who we really are and what we really believe. Our words are our responsibility. They are a chance to connect. And if they aren't driven by love and concern for other people then we probably need to hush up.

Thank you all, once again, for your very valuable time. You show up to hear me tell stories, you read my words and you laugh with me (and at me—which is absolutely fine and dandy) and you value my work.

It means more than you'll ever know.

www.thealabamahousewife.com

Made in the USA
Columbia, SC
12 April 2023

15281747R00126